BARBRA
STREISAND

WILLIAM RUHLMANN

LONGMEADOW
PRESS

Published by Longmeadow Press,
201 High Ridge Road, Stamford,
CT 06904. All rights reserved. No
part of this book may be
reproduced or utilized in any form
or by any means, electronic or
mechanical, including
photocopying, recording or by any
information storage and retrieval
system, without permission in
writing from the copyright owner.

Longmeadow Press and the
colophon are registered
trademarks.

ISBN 0-681-10102-4

Printed in Slovenia

First Longmeadow Press Edition

0 9 8 7 6 5 4 3 2 1

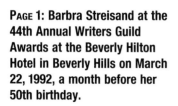

**PAGE 1: Barbra Streisand at the
44th Annual Writers Guild
Awards at the Beverly Hilton
Hotel in Beverly Hills on March
22, 1992, a month before her
50th birthday.**

**PREVIOUS PAGE: With Broadway
composer Stephen Sondheim,
backstage at the Grammy
Awards Show, holding her
Grammy Living Legends
Award, February 25, 1992. "I
don't feel like a legend," she
said. "I feel like a work in
progress."**

**RIGHT: At the Director's Guild of
America Awards, March 26,
1986.**

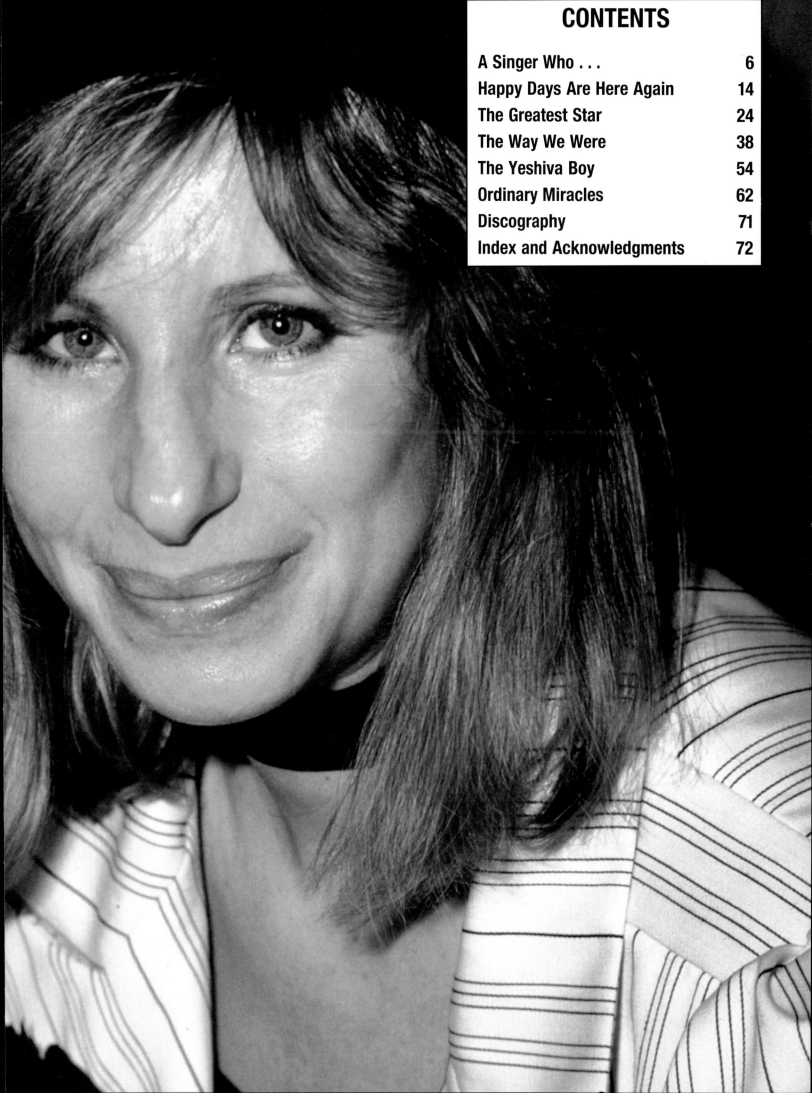

CONTENTS

A SINGER WHO . . .

Barbra Streisand is the most accomplished popular singer of her generation. That statement is impressive enough in itself, but instead of being the definitive superlative about her career, it is just a simple fact that only begins to define Streisand's significance in the post-World War II era that she has dominated.

It takes a series of other facts to trace the outlines of Streisand's impact on popular music. In a long recording career, Streisand has released around 40 albums, and contributed to cast and soundtrack records. As of 1993, these releases had resulted in 36 gold albums (signifying sales of half a million copies), of which 22 are also platinum (a million copies) and seven multi-platinum. In total, she has sold more than 60 million albums.

Streisand's popularity as a recording artist can also be measured by chart success, as measured by *Billboard* magazine. She has hit *Billboard*'s album charts with 44 records (including cast and soundtrack albums), and their success up to 1992 was enough to place her at #5 among the top album artists since 1955. The records have also been honored by the recording industry. Streisand has won seven

ABOVE: Barbra Streisand, shooting a video for "Somewhere," returns to the bare lightbulb and worn floors of the Broadway stage, 1985.

RIGHT: The first time around, in another antique dress.

Grammy Awards as well as a Lifetime Achievement Award.

But even these facts and figures give only a partial portrait of Streisand's triumph as a singer. To fill in the picture, one must consider her career in the context of the times in which she has lived and her own personal approach to her work.

Any artist functioning in a popular medium over time must contend with the vagaries of trends and fashions. But no popular singer in history has swum so determinedly and successfully against the tide as Streisand. Nineteen sixty-two, the year her first recordings were released, was an interim period in popular music. The first wave of rock 'n' roll had struck and receded, shaking up the singles charts, but leaving album sales largely in the hands of adults who favored show music and the "classic pop" singers who had emerged or descended from the big bands of the swing era.

But the onset of the British "invasion" in 1964 began to change everything, and soon rock came to dominate popular

music, leaving all else behind. Unlike nearly all her peers, Streisand was not wiped out by that second wave. She made occasional attempts to accommodate it, but for the most part she simply withstood it until, in the '70s, she was able to become part of a new pop music that incorporated elements of rock without eliminating the lyrical and melodic strengths of earlier music.

As a result, Streisand is the only consistently successful non-rock singer of the rock era. No wonder that in 1992 she signed a new contract with Sony Music Entertainment (which includes the Columbia Records label and Columbia Pictures)

worth a reported $60 million, an amount in the range of such '90s superstars as Madonna and Michael Jackson.

Streisand's remarkable recording career also must be judged in the context of the artist's own relatively reduced estimation of it among her priorities. You might expect that anyone who had achieved what Streisand has in music could only have done so by focusing all her energies on it, by performing extensively and devoting most of her time to her musical career. Instead, Streisand has always taken her singing for granted, insisting that she was interested primarily in being an actress, and, later, a film director.

And, of course, she has found considerable success apart from her singing. Streisand has appeared in two Broadway shows and received a Tony Award as "Star of the Decade" for the 1960s. She has made five network television specials (plus three for cable) and won Emmys. She has acted in 15 films, winning the Academy Award for Best Actress. She was involved as a producer in five of those films, she directed two of them and she co-wrote the screenplay for one. "Evergreen (Love Theme From 'A Star Is Born')," which she co-wrote, won a Grammy as Song of the Year and an Oscar as Best Original Song from a motion picture. And she composed the score for her 1987 film *Nuts*.

Because of the widespread fame associated with movie stardom, Streisand has tended to be judged more for her film work than her music. One biography of her was entitled *An Actress Who Sings*, echoing her own definition of herself, and many observers have taken her estimation as correct. It isn't. Despite her success in the movies, Streisand remains what she always has been: a singer who acts (and writes and produces and directs). Take away that remarkable, one-of-a-kind voice, and you might have – given Streisand's legendary persistence and hard work – a moderately successful character actress, or – given her legendary perfectionism and uncooperativeness – someone who never made it beyond the lower echelons of struggling New York actresses.

But with the voice, a character actress becomes a leading lady, and an obnoxious pest becomes a temperamental star. If any more proof were needed that the public sees Streisand primarily as a singer, the amazing response to her return to the concert stage in 1994 provided it.

That's not to say, however, that one can really divorce Barbra Streisand the singer from Barbra Streisand the actress. If the instrument is amazing in itself, the personality that uses it is just as stunning, shaping a song into a unique performance at least as expressive of the singer's identity as the songwriter's intentions. In fact, usually more so. Streisand frequently has been criticized for overpowering her material

and, especially in her early days, the criticism had some truth. But it is also fair to say that no singer has done so much for mediocre material.

This is perhaps the most remarkable, and least discussed, aspect of Streisand's remarkable career. It wasn't just that she came along when popular music was about to veer off in a direction she would not choose to follow. It was that she entered a style of popular music in decline and fashioned a career out of its cast-offs, also-rans and second-rate talents. Unlike the classic pop singers who preceded her, she did not, for the most part, sing the music of the great songwriters of the pre-World War II era. Only rarely did she perform the songs of George Gershwin, Cole Porter, Irving Berlin, and the rest.

LEFT: As Dolly Levi in *Hello, Dolly!*, her second film role, shot in 1968.

RIGHT: At the Directors Guild of America Awards at the Beverly Hilton Hotel, Beverly Hills, March 14, 1992, where she was nominated for Best Director for *The Prince Of Tides*. She was only the third woman ever nominated.

RIGHT: **Brother and sister Sheldon and Barbra Streisand flank half-sister Roslyn Kind during Kind's appearance at the Grand Finale nightclub in New York, November 1977.**

Instead, when it came to show music, she sang the songs of Harold Rome, of Jule Styne and Bob Merrill, of Jerry Herman. And in her films, she worked with the likes of Michel Legrand and Marilyn and Alan Bergman, a songwriting team she adopted as completely as Frank Sinatra had Sammy Cahn and Jimmy Van Heusen.

Most pop singers have been stymied by the decline in traditional songwriting since the '60s. Streisand has reveled in it, able to take a bland Legrand-Bergman tune and remake it, breathing in all the feeling and sophistication, all the musical power, the song-as-written lacked. She is equaled only perhaps by Sinatra in her ability to hide the weaknesses of a merely average song by giving it a transfusion of her own talent.

Few artists can be as precisely located in a cultural milieu, not to mention a neighborhood, as Barbra Joan Streisand. (The second ''a'' in her first name was dropped in her early days as an actress: characteristically, she wanted to direct people how to pronounce her name.) She was born on Pulaski Street in the Williamsburg section of Brooklyn, New York, the second child of a kosher Jewish family, on April 24, 1942.

From her parents she inherited both intellect and singing ability. Her maternal grandfather, a garment cutter, was a cantor at his synagogue, and her mother, Diana Rosen Streisand, had singing and theatrical ambitions. Her father, Emmanuel Streisand, taught high school English and Psychology.

The family's middle-class status was shattered in August

1943 when Emmanuel Streisand died suddenly at the age of 35. Diana Streisand and her two children moved back in with her parents and were supported by her job as a bookkeeper. In 1949, Diana married real estate dealer Louis Kind. (The couple would separate permanently, however, by 1956.)

Streisand's dreams of being a movie actress came early. But so did the hope of a singing career. Inspired by her favorite singer, Joni James, a 10-year-old Streisand got an audition at James's label, MGM Records, where she sang James's hit, ''Have You Heard.'' Nothing came of it.

Streisand graduated from P.S. 89 in 1955 and went on to Erasmus Hall High School. In December, she went to a private recording studio and came out with a rendition of ''You'll Never Know.'' Preserved on her 1991 boxed set *Just For The Record . . .* , it reveals a singer with a pure tone who is already taking chances with phrasing and breath placement.

In April 1956, Streisand went to see the Pulitzer prize-winning play *The Diary Of Anne Frank.* The 14-year-old's desire to be an actress was solidified by watching Susan Strasberg play the title role, if only because she thought she could have played the part much better.

Though Streisand graduated from Erasmus in January 1959 with a 93 average, she did not consider going on to college. She got a job across the river in Manhattan as a switchboard operator and, when she'd saved enough money, moved into an apartment and began the age-old journey of the aspiring actress, taking acting classes and working at more menial jobs in the theater.

HAPPY DAYS ARE HERE AGAIN

RIGHT: As Miss Marmelstein in *I Can Get It For You Wholesale*, 1962. Streisand insisted on performing her featured song seated. (She rolled out onstage.) The audience stood instead, and applauded wildly.

NEXT PAGE: Streisand in 1963, around the time she revealed her "secret" marriage to Elliott Gould. Actually, they wouldn't marry until September, but she was already wearing a wedding ring during a nightclub engagement in May.

Over the next year, Streisand struggled, living on unemployment while going to auditions, eventually, at the urging of friends, even ones that required singing. In May 1960, she got a role in a show called *The Insect Comedy* that ran three nights off Off-Broadway. In the show she met an aspiring actor, Barry Dennen, who encouraged her to sing and played her the records in his collection (including, though she would later allegedly deny any familiarity with them, those of singer/comedienne Fanny Brice).

Dennen, who lived on Ninth Street, across from a bar called the Lion, also suggested that Streisand enter the bar's amateur contest, at which, in June, she beat three other contestants by singing "A Sleepin' Bee," a song by Truman Capote and Harold Arlen from the musical *House Of Flowers*. The prize was $50 and a week's engagement. Thus began Barbra Streisand's career as a cabaret singer.

Following her week at the Lion, Streisand auditioned at the tonier Bon Soir nightclub and was hired for two weeks in September. The engagement ended up being extended into December. During this period, she acquired her first manager,

Ted Rozar, who was able to book her out of town, and she played in Detroit and St. Louis in March and April 1961.

It wasn't only the voice that drew the customers. It was Streisand's look, an amalgamation of period clothes from second-hand shops, and it was her personality, full of a self-knowing humor. There was also her unusual repertoire, which featured such songs as "Who's Afraid Of The Big Bad Wolf," an uptempo arrangement of "Lover, Come Back To Me," and "Cry Me A River," the song popularized by Julie London, who sang it as a melodramatic weeper, while Streisand turned it into a song of savage vengeance.

Streisand's relationship with Rozar proved volatile, and she soon turned to a new manager, Marty Erlichman, whose major clients were the Irish group The Clancy Brothers and Tommy Makem. They were signed to Columbia Records, and Erlichman therefore was able to get Streisand a hearing from the company's president, Goddard Lieberson. Lieberson met with Streisand, listened to a tape of a performance at the Bon Soir, acknowledged that she had talent, and turned her down.

Meanwhile, Streisand had not given up her aspirations in the

ABOVE: Elliott Gould, Jack Kruschen and Barbra Streisand in a scene from *I Can Get It For You Wholesale*. "Miss Streisand," reported UPI, "who has aroused much enthusiasm in her first assault on Broadway, will probably spend the rest of her professional life fighting for the spelling of her first name in public print."

ABOVE, RIGHT: Unknown, actor Eli Wallach, Streisand, and director Elia Kazan at the presentation of *Cue* magazine's Entertainer of the Year Award to Streisand, December 27, 1963.

LEFT: With *Funny Girl* producer Ray Stark at the premiere of the *Funny Girl* film at the Criterion Theatre, September 18, 1968.

theater. In August, she auditioned for an Off-Broadway revue called *Another Evening With Harry Stoones*. She got a part, and the show opened and closed on October 21.

On the day after Thanksgiving, Streisand auditioned for a Broadway musical called *I Can Get It For You Wholesale*, based on a novel by Jerome Weidman about an opportunistic man in the New York garment trade. There was really no part for a 19-year-old female singer/comedienne, but the production team was so impressed by Streisand that they altered and beefed up the part of Miss Marmelstein, a spinster secretary, so that Streisand could play it.

On March 22, 1962, when *I Can Get It For You Wholesale* opened, Streisand stole the show, singing a lament named after her character, and the musical became a hit. As a result, on April 1, she joined the rest of the cast for the recording of the cast album, which was to be released on Columbia Records. The producer of the album was Goddard Lieberson. But Streisand still didn't get her own contract.

On May 29, Streisand appeared on "The Gary Moore Show" on CBS-TV as part of the show's regular "wonderful year" segment, which, on this occasion, commemorated the year 1929. Ken Welch of the show had Streisand sing "Happy Days Are Here Again," which Franklin Roosevelt had used as a campaign song in 1932, in a tremendously effective slow arrangement. The show was caught by Columbia A&R director David Kapralik, who was one of the people Marty Erlichman

had been badgering to sign Streisand. He was converted on the spot and began trying to get Lieberson to give Streisand a recording contract.

Finally, on October 1, 1962, Barbra Streisand signed to Columbia Records. She was paid a $20,000 advance. The only unusual aspects about the contract were that it gave Streisand the right to pick her own material and that it guaranteed her an album release. The latter was especially notable since new artists generally didn't get to release LPs until succeeding with a single or two. The clause would prove to be Streisand's salvation.

On October 16, Streisand recorded her first single, "Happy Days Are Here Again." Though Columbia released the single at the end of the month, the label doesn't seem to have put much faith in it, reportedly pressing only 500 copies. It didn't chart, nor did her second single, "My Coloring Book."

All this time, Streisand continued to appear in *I Can Get It For You Wholesale* as well as performing late-night club engagements. The pace let up a little on December 9, when the show closed. But in December and January, Streisand was hard at work picking songs and preparing for the album guaranteed by her contract.

The sessions for the album were held on January 23, 24 and 25, 1963. To a large extent, it recreated one of Streisand's club shows, with slightly fleshed-out orchestrations. The 11 selections included "A Sleepin' Bee," "Cry Me A River,"

LEFT: Streisand poses with Jule Styne (at piano) and Bob Merrill, the songwriting team for *Funny Girl*, in February 1964, shortly before the show's Broadway opening.

RIGHT: Backstage at *Funny Girl*, the Winter Garden, opening night, March 26, 1964. Streisand's visitors are Fanny Brice's brother Lew (left), her daughter Fran (Mrs. Ray Stark), and her son William.

"Who's Afraid Of The Big, Bad Wolf?" and "Happy Days Are Here Again," as well as two obscure songs by well-known '30s songwriters: "I'll Tell The Man In The Street," a Richard Rodgers-Lorenz Hart tune, and "Come To The Supermarket (In Old Peking)," a late Cole Porter song.

Released in February, *The Barbra Streisand Album* was well-received critically. "Miss Streisand is a compelling stylist with a full, rich vocal quality that may give you goosebumps when you hear her more dramatic arias," wrote Stanley Green in *Hi Fi/Stereo Review* magazine. "She has a sure control and knows what she is doing at all times." Significantly, Green was not impressed with "the supposedly comic numbers," preferring the big-voiced ballad singer in Streisand. But the album actually de-emphasized Streisand's humorous side,

and for most listeners this would be their first exposure to her.

Streisand embarked on a national nightclub tour in March to promote the album. Though she could have played more upscale rooms, Erlichman booked her into hip, bohemian clubs like the Hungry i in San Francisco and Mr. Kelly's in Chicago. She also played a three-week engagement at the Eden Roc Hotel in Miami and appeared at Basin Street East in New York.

The Barbra Streisand Album entered *Billboard*'s Top LP chart for the week ending April 13. It would rise to #8, and its total chart run would last almost two years.

While it was high in the charts, Streisand was busy recording its follow-up, which she started on June 3. Having debuted with Harold Arlen's "A Sleepin' Bee" three years before, she very nearly dedicated her second LP to the composer, performing his songs "Any Place I Hang My Hat Is Home," "Right As The Rain," "Down With Love," "When The Sun Comes Out," and "Like A Straw In The Wind." Other songs, such as "Lover, Come Back To Me" and "I Stayed Too Long At The Fair," were from Streisand's nightclub act, while "My Coloring Book" was retrieved from her second single.

Now remembered as of a piece with her first and third albums in an early trilogy, *The Second Barbra Streisand Album* occasioned the first notable negative critical comments in Streisand's recording career. For all those bowled over by her vocal gifts, there always would be a minority not only unmoved, but somewhat annoyed. Their view is well expressed by John F. Indcox, who reviewed the second LP in *High Fidelity* magazine. Acknowledging that he had liked her first album, Indcox nevertheless reports that "her work here is pretentiously arty, overinvolved and overprojected and made further intolerable by a vocal tone best described by the Irish word 'keening.'" Streisand's new record-buying following did not share Indcox's view. Released in August, while the singer was spending two weeks opening for Liberace in Las Vegas, *The Second Barbra Streisand Album* would hit #2 on the charts during a 74-week run.

On September 13, in Carson City, Nevada, Streisand married actor Elliott Gould, whom she had met when he was the lead in *I Can Get It For You Wholesale*. Gould was beginning to make a name for himself in the theater, but he would not become a major star until the late '60s and early '70s, when he had a run of successful films.

Streisand, on the other hand, was becoming the big discovery of 1963. When she had turned up at "The Ed Sullivan Show" for her appearance on June 9, she hadn't been recognized by a security guard. But when she appeared on "The Judy Garland Show" on October 6, she managed to upstage the star, and her mocking question, "Can I replace you?" sounded all too honest. For many, Streisand *was* the

new Garland, the new Ethel Merman (also on the show), or even the new Fanny Brice.

It's no wonder, then, that Streisand was cast as Brice in the Broadway musical based on her life and "presented" (i.e., produced) by her son-in-law, Ray Stark. Stark had been trying to make a film called *My Man* (the title of Brice's signature song) for years, later deciding to do it first as a show. It was one of those projects that went through many composers, directors, and stars before the principals finally settled on director Garson Kanin and the songwriting team of Jule Styne and Bob Merrill. By 1963, Streisand was an obvious choice for the lead, and Styne even wrote many of the songs with her in mind.

In retrospect, it's hard to imagine anyone else doing the part, though Anne Bancroft was originally announced for it. A more interesting question is why a singer near the top of the charts, who was now getting nearly five figures for a night of work, would want to return to the theater and do eight shows a week for considerably less.

Just as Streisand's appropriateness for the lead in what was now called *Funny Girl* seems obvious, so now her use of the

BELOW: **Streisand as Fanny Brice in *Funny Girl* on Broadway.**

NEXT PAGE: **Streisand and Sydney Chaplin (as Nicky Arnstein) onstage at the Winter Garden in *Funny Girl*.**

show as a stepping stone to stardom also seems logical. But at the point in her career when she took the job, it was a deliberate step back. She even signed a run-of-the-show contract, keeping her in New York indefinitely and thus abandoning the lucrative concert circuit that could have brought her millions in the wake of her successful albums.

It was, however, a typical career decision for Streisand. It reflected long-term rather than short-term goals; it was risky; and it showed a desire to move on. Throughout her career, whenever Streisand has conquered a particular aspect of show business, she has abandoned it rather than consolidating that success, and moved on to a new challenge.

This is not to say that Streisand abandoned recording, although she would approach it differently hereafter. She did find time, while preparing for *Funny Girl*, to record a third album, appropriately called *The Third Album*. But it was perhaps the least interesting of the three. Two new arrangers, Ray Ellis and Sid Ramin, were brought in, and the song selection was far more conventional, turning to such familiar material as "Taking A Chance On Love" and "As Time Goes By."

The Third Album became Streisand's third straight Top 10 hit, though it only reached #5, perhaps because it had to fight its way through the newly emergent Beatles. Nevertheless, its 74 weeks in the charts matched the second album's total.

Columbia seemed to have given up on the singles market, releasing no 45s from Streisand's first three albums. But Capitol Records had rights to the *Funny Girl* cast album, while Columbia, due to its contract with Streisand, had obtained the right to release singles of songs from the show. On January 21, 1964, while *Funny Girl* was in out-of-town tryouts, Columbia released a Streisand 45 pairing two of the musical's songs, "I Am Woman" and "People." Initially, it flopped.

Funny Girl opened on Broadway on March 26, and in its issue for the week ending March 28, *Billboard* listed both sides of the single (which Columbia had now reserviced and was promoting to radio) on its Bubbling Under The Hot 100 chart. "I Am Woman," originally intended to be the A-side, faded, but "People" reached #100 the following week, becoming Streisand's first entry on the "Hot 100."

It still was not an immediate hit, however. It rose to #97, then dropped to #99, before gaining a "bullet" and rising to #84 for the week ending April 25, 1964. By that time, Streisand had appeared on the cover of *Time* magazine, *Funny Girl* was an established hit, and Capitol had released its cast album. The album entered the *Billboard* LP chart for the week ending May 2, the same week that Columbia's "People" bulletted to #62. The single finally peaked at #5, while the cast album got to #2.

LEFT: **Streisand cuts the cake at the farewell party after her final performance onstage in** *Funny Girl*, **London, July 16, 1966. She was in her fourth month of pregnancy.**

RIGHT: **With husband Elliott Gould at the opening night party for** *Funny Girl*, **the early hours of March 27, 1964, at the Rainbow Room, Rockefeller Center, New York.**

The show, meanwhile, turned out to be a perfect vehicle for Streisand's talents. Possessed of an uneven book, it fictionalized Fanny Brice's life story, telling of her rise to fame in the theater, coincident with her crumbling marriage to gambler Nicky Arnstein. The score also was uneven, but in "People," "I'm The Greatest Star" and "Don't Rain On My Parade," it gave Streisand showstopping material.

It was also easy to see the star as telling her own story, not Brice's. "I'm The Greatest Star" seemed to be what Barbra Streisand had been telling the world all along, and one could even point to certain parallels between her personal life – with a less-famous husband who loved to gamble – and that of Fanny Brice. In any case, Streisand would be associated with the character permanently, especially after making a movie version of the musical, and later film projects also would show echoes of it.

"Barbra Streisand was a Grammy godsend when she burst into the scene in 1963," writes Henry Schipper in his book *Broken Record: The Inside Story Of The Grammy Awards*. The Grammys, founded by the conservative wing of the record business as a bulwark against rock 'n' roll in the late '50s, and

lately buffetted by the British invasion, welcomed Barbra Streisand with open arms when it finally got around to giving out its 1963 awards on May 12, 1964. *The Barbra Streisand Album*, released 15 months earlier, won Album of the Year, and Streisand won Best Vocal Performance, Female. It was a big day: Streisand also received her first gold record for *The Second Barbra Streisand Album*.

Columbia followed up Streisand's first Top 10 single by titling her fourth album after it. *People* was released in September 1964. The album's songs, which included selections by such theater music composers as Styne and Merrill, Cy Coleman and Carolyn Leigh, Irving Berlin, Jerry Bock and Sheldon Harnick, Rodgers and Hammerstein, Richard Maltby, Jr., and David Shire, and Arlen and Capote, didn't so much consist of inspired discoveries as minor works, given greater significance by Streisand's readings.

Of course, the LP also included the title track, and that was enough to send it to #1 on the charts. Streisand was at a popular peak. During one week in October, *Cash Box* magazine listed all four Streisand albums, plus the *Funny Girl* cast album, among its 100 best-sellers.

THE GREATEST STAR

All this time, of course, it was possible to go to the Winter Garden Theater and see America's biggest recording star live on stage. But though a full-time recording career and eight performances in a Broadway show would have been more than enough for most people, Streisand branched out into another field. In June 1964, she had signed with CBS-TV for a group of television specials. The decision to do specials rather than a series was a typically shrewd one. Doubtless, Streisand could have gotten much more than the mere $5 million over 10 years the specials called for by doing a regular weekly series. But though TV has demonstrated an enormous promotional power for singers, those who have appeared on it week in and week out generally have suffered overexposure and resulting career slumps. Streisand's contract assured that her appearances on TV would be events, not typical fare.

On April 13, 1965, Streisand won her second Best Vocal Performance, Female, Grammy for the *People* LP. The album also garnered two other Grammys: Peter Matz won the Best Accompaniment for Vocalist(s) or Instrumentalist(s), and art director Robert Cato and photographer Don Bronstein won for Best Album Cover. (Streisand had insisted on the cover, which

showed her standing on a beach with her back to the camera, over the strenuous objections of Columbia's marketing staff.) Jule Styne and Bob Merrill, meanwhile, won the Best Score from an Original Cast Show Album Grammy for *Funny Girl*.

Streisand's first TV special, "My Name Is Barbra," was broadcast on April 28. A one-hour program without guest stars, it featured Streisand performing 20 numbers in a variety of guises, from five-year-old child to adult concert performer. Structured in three segments – an *Alice In Wonderland* sequence, a medley of down-and-out songs, and a live set – it reprised songs from her nightclub act and from *Funny Girl* and allowed her to try out "My Man" for the first time.

The show garnered high ratings. It was America's first chance to see the famous Broadway and recording star at length and judge not only her acting and singing talent, but also her appearance on camera. Many performers had conquered the record charts and/or Broadway without crossing over to TV and film. "My Name Is Barbra" offered evidence that Streisand had the potential to do so. When TV's Emmy Awards were given out on September 12, the show won five, including Outstanding Individual Achievement in

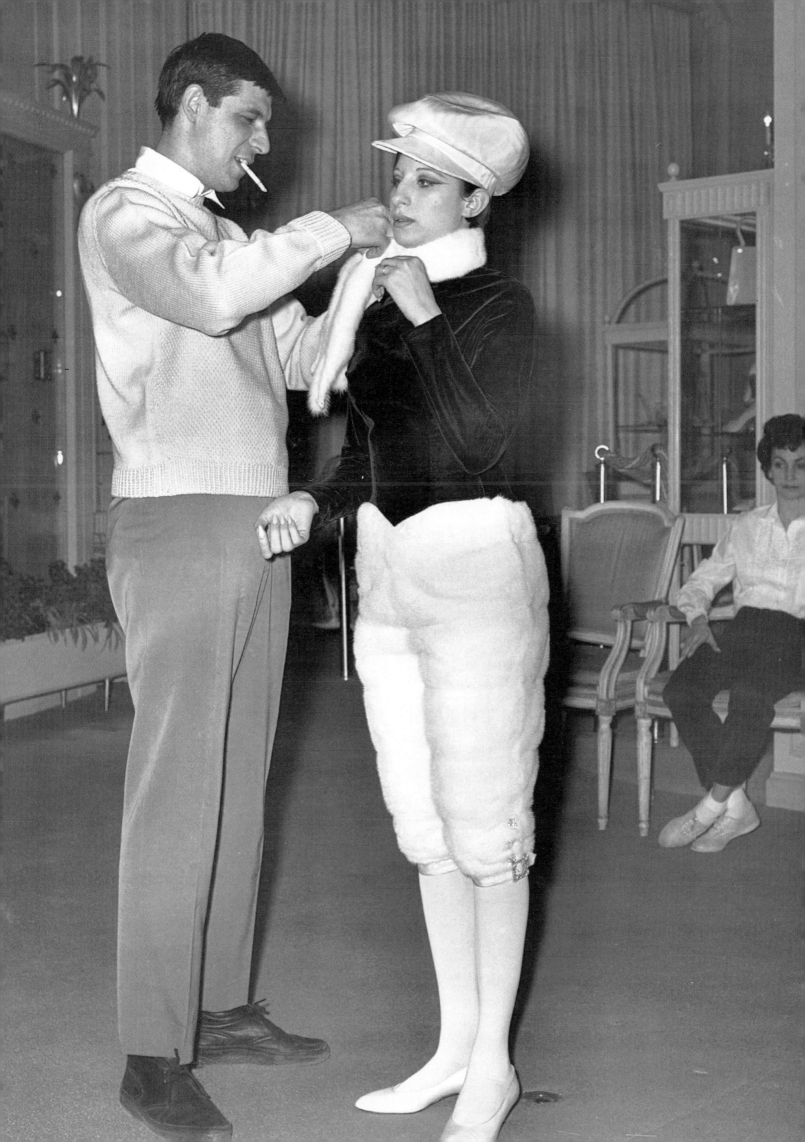

Entertainment for Streisand herself.

The week after the special, Columbia had a *My Name Is Barbra* album in the record stores, though the LP is only a partial soundtrack to the TV show, with just six of its 12 tracks having been featured. It was an enormous hit during the summer of 1965, reaching #2; it stayed in the charts 68 weeks and went gold on December 2.

On September 13, Columbia released "He Touched Me" as a single in advance of the next Streisand album, *My Name Is Barbra, Two . . . .* The song, as well as the single's non-LP B-side, "I Like Him," were from *Drat! The Cat!*, a musical that opened on Broadway on October 10 and closed a week later. It starred Elliott Gould. "He Touched Me" only got to #53. But *My Name Is Barbra, Two . . .* did much better when it was released in October. The album, which included three previously unissued numbers from the TV special along with eight newly recorded tracks, soared to #2. Columbia released ''Second Hand Rose'' from the album as a single in November. The song had been introduced by Fanny Brice. In the TV special, it had provided an occasion for Streisand to romp through Bergdorf-Goodman's department store; on record, it showed off her comedic gifts. In early 1966, it became her second Top 40 hit, rising to #32.

Streisand finished playing Fanny Brice on Broadway when she left *Funny Girl* in December 1965. She would return to the role more than once, however.

On March 15, 1966, Streisand won her third consecutive Best Vocal Performance, Female, Grammy for *My Name Is Barbra*. Surprisingly, it would be her last Grammy for many years.

Her second TV special, ''Color Me Barbra,'' was broadcast on March 30. (Color was a relatively new feature of television broadcasting; the first special had been in black and white.) Structurally similar to the first, it featured the star singing to the artwork in the Philadelphia Museum, to the animals in a studio zoo, and finally to an audience. Like her first special, it earned high ratings and critical approval.

There was also, of course, a soundtrack album released concurrent with the special, its highlights including Rodgers and Hart's ''Where Or When'' and Maltby and Shire's ''Starting Here, Starting Now.'' The album hit #3 and was certified Streisand's seventh straight gold album within weeks of its release.

On April 13, Streisand opened in *Funny Girl* in London for a 14-week run, repeating the good notices and box office of her New York success. Shortly afterward, she and Gould announced that she was pregnant, and when the run was over on July 14, she played four shows of a scheduled concert tour of the U.S., but then retired temporarily to await the birth of her child. She would not embark on another national concert tour for 28 years.

The retirement did not apply to recordings, however. In late October, Columbia released *Je M'Appelle Barbra*, on which

Streisand sang effectively in both French and English. The album hit #5, but it stayed in the charts only 29 weeks and was her first album not to achieve a gold certification.

But Streisand had other concerns. On December 29, she gave birth to a son, Jason Emmanuel Gould. By late April 1967, she was back at work, preparing her third TV special, a conceptual work called "The Belle Of 14th Street" that co-starred actor Jason Robards, Jr. It was not immediately scheduled for broadcast, however.

On May 10, Streisand arrived in Hollywood to work on the film version of *Funny Girl*. Such Broadway stars as Ethel Merman, Mary Martin, and Julie Andrews (before her film breakthrough with *Mary Poppins*) had been denied the chance to recreate their stage triumphs on film, but Streisand, by extending her appeal with records and television work, was able to walk into Hollywood with a starring role in her first picture.

During the filming, Streisand returned to New York for a weekend in June and appeared in a free concert in Central Park before 135,000 people. The show was recorded and filmed, though, like "The Belle Of 14th Street," the results were shelved for the moment.

Columbia released two Streisand albums in October. *Simply Streisand* contained more standards than any of her previous records – "My Funny Valentine," "Lover Man," "More Than You Know," "All The Things You Are" – but standards were not what Streisand was known for or did best. "The truth is that this is a transition album," wrote Morgan Ames in *High Fidelity*. "Miss Streisand knows where she's been, but she's undecided about where she's going." Some Streisand fans weren't willing to go with her: *Simply Streisand*, peaking at #12, became her first album to miss the Top 10.

The other October release was *A Christmas Album*, a combination of sacred and celebratory seasonal songs that was among the best in the genre. It topped the Christmas chart in December and would become a perennial seller. By the 1992 Christmas season, it had sold over three million copies.

Also in October, CBS-TV broadcast "The Belle Of 14th Street." It was universally condemned by critics, typical of whom was Jack Gould in *The New York Times*, who called it "an embarrassing outing, a concoction of deranged

LEFT: Streisand onstage for the first time in 10 months, appearing in a free concert in Central Park, New York, June 17, 1967.

BELOW: Some of the 135,000 people who showed up in Sheeps Meadow, Central Park, for Barbra Streisand's free concert.

29

productions that not even the star and her major colleague of the evening, Jason Robards, could straighten out." Unlike "My Name Is Barbra" and "Color Me Barbra," the show did not produce a soundtrack album, and it has not been issued on home video.

With her stage career over, her record company temporarily sated by the recent release of two LPs, her TV career damaged by "The Belle Of 14th Street," and her first film assignment finished by December, Streisand, following the holidays and a vacation, began a second motion picture in February 1968. Strangely enough, it was *Hello, Dolly!*, the other hit of the 1963-1964 Broadway season. Carol Channing, who originated the role of Dolly Levi in this musicalized version of Thornton Wilder's play *The Matchmaker*, had won a Tony Award over Streisand. Now, Streisand was beating out Channing for the movie role, especially unusual because the story called for a much older woman.

By 1968, Columbia Records President Clive Davis had been won over by the rock revolution. He was convinced not only that his company's future lay in recording new rock talent like Big Brother and the Holding Company (who he had signed after hearing them at the Monterey Pop Festival in June 1967),

but that Columbia's roster of pop and jazz stars should accommodate rock into their styles to maintain or increase their sales. In Davis's view, the recent Streisand albums *Je M'Appelle Barbra* and *Simply Streisand* (which had sold about 350,000 copies each) hadn't faltered because they failed to match the standard of her earlier work, but because the record-buying public was shifting and no longer cared to hear the "old" Streisand.

Davis showed up on the set of *Hello, Dolly!* and talked to Streisand about trying to "contemporize" her image by singing the songs of young, current songwriters with rock-like arrangements. Streisand resisted, but ultimately would give in to the idea.

She finished shooting *Hello, Dolly!*, which had turned out to be a difficult, expensive production, in August. On August 8, Columbia released the movie soundtrack to *Funny Girl*. It differed considerably from the cast album, dropping eight songs and adding a few others, among them a new title song and two songs associated with Fanny Brice, "I'd Rather Be Blue" and "My Man." As became apparent on September 18 when the film opened, director William Wyler, a respected Hollywood veteran who had never directed a musical, was less

LEFT: Rehearsing with Jason Robards for her third TV special, "The Belle of 14th Street," which was shelved for six months, then broadcast in October 1967 to poor notices.

ABOVE: Four Broadway divas, Beatrice Lillie (of *High Spirits*), Sally Ann Howes of *What Makes Sammy Run*, Streisand, and Carol Channing of *Hello, Dolly!*, pose with Lynda Bird Johnson (second from right), daughter of the President, on a visit to New York, February 20, 1965.

RIGHT: Walter Scharf, musical director of the film version of *Funny Girl*, works with Streisand on the soundtrack.

LEFT: Streisand with director Gene Kelly on the set of *Hello, Dolly!*, July 1968.

RIGHT: Streisand sings "People" with Omar Sharif (as Nicky Arnstein) in the film version of *Funny Girl*.

interested in the musical numbers (which were directed by Herbert Ross) than the dramatic scenes. As a result, *Funny Girl* on film was a more downbeat, less musical work than it had been onstage.

Happily, both versions had the same thing going for them: Barbra Streisand. Her critical notices were universally positive, and the film was a major hit of the fall season. The soundtrack album hit #12, went gold, and stayed in the charts more than two years.

The success of the film overshadowed the belated appearance of Streisand's June 1967 Central Park concert on TV and record. "A Happening In Central Park" aired on September 15, 1968, simultaneous with the release of a Columbia album of the performance. The show was well-received by critics and got good ratings. But the album only reached #30, Streisand's lowest chart peak ever.

In October, Streisand began rehearsals for her third big-budget movie musical, *On A Clear Day You Can See Forever*, about a contemporary New York woman with ESP and hyperkinetic powers who discovers her past lives while

undergoing hypnosis to cure her of cigarette smoking. The film began shooting in January 1969.

In February, Streisand and Elliott Gould announced that they were separating. They would divorce in 1971. In other news, it was announced that Streisand had signed to appear for four weeks, once a year for five years, at the Las Vegas International Hotel, for which she would be paid $125,000 a week.

Also in February, Streisand was nominated for Best Actress for *Funny Girl* in the Academy Awards; against stiff competition, she tied with Katharine Hepburn in winning the Oscar at the ceremonies held on April 14.

Streisand completed filming *On A Clear Day* in the late spring of 1969, just in time to make her first engagement in Las Vegas in July.

Streisand biographer Rene Jordan suggests that she had not at this point entirely given up the idea of returning to the stage, citing a proposed show about actress Sarah Bernhardt. He says, however, that Streisand now shied away from signing the kind of run-of-the-play contract that had kept her in *Funny Girl* for two years. Nevertheless, he reports, Streisand did make herself up to look like Bernhardt for the cover of her next album.

It was an odd choice for an LP on which Streisand finally was dipping her toe into rock music. You certainly wouldn't know by looking at the curly haired, heavily made-up face on the cover of *What About Today?* that it featured Streisand's takes on the Beatles and other contemporary writers. Actually,

FAR LEFT: French actor/singer Maurice Chevalier and his lively date at the Paris premiere of *Funny Girl*, January 1969.

LEFT: In her Scassi pajama dress at the Academy Awards with Elliot Gould, April 14, 1969, where she won as Best Actress for *Funny Girl*, tieing with Katharine Hepburn.

LEFT, BELOW: At the "Broadway For Peace" show at Avery Fisher Hall, Lincoln Center, New York, January 21, 1968.

RIGHT: Streisand in Central Park during the filming of *On A Clear Day You Can See Forever*, summer 1969.

the album was only a half-hearted updating that relied on such old standbys as Harold Arlen and Maltby and Shire, and looked more toward the new, non-rock pop of Jimmy Webb, Burt Bacharach and Hal David, and the team of Alan and Marilyn Bergman and Michel Legrand, soon to become Streisand's house songwriters.

Whether it was the cover or the selections, however, *What About Today?* failed to reverse Streisand's decline in record sales, hitting only #31, though it did stay in the charts 40 weeks.

Streisand, meanwhile, began filming a non-singing role in the comedy *The Owl And The Pussycat* in October in New

York City. It was her fourth straight film to be based on a Broadway production, this one a 1964 play about a New York prostitute and a bookstore clerk.

You may recall that, back in 1968, Streisand had made a movie called *Hello, Dolly!* Ever since, it had sat on the shelf, the victim of a contract agreement that provided no film of the show would be released while it was still running on Broadway, or until the start of 1971, whichever came first. That had seemed like a good deal in 1964, but by 1969, especially due to an all-black cast led by Pearl Bailey, *Hello, Dolly!* was still running. Finally, however, producer David Merrick relented and allowed the movie to open in December 1969.

As far as critics were concerned, he needn't have bothered. By 1969, the era of the big, splashy Broadway musical on film was long gone, and *Hello, Dolly!*, the most expensive musical made up to that time, was an anachronism. It was not a complete disaster at the box office, that is only to say that it did not, as had been feared, lead 20th Century-Fox into bankruptcy. In fact, if it had been made with an average

budget, it would have been a hit. But when you spend $24 million on a movie and only make $15 million back, you're more than $9 million in the hole, counting costs of prints and advertising. (Hollywood rule-of-thumb is that a film's gross must double its production cost to show a profit.)

Some of Streisand's notices were positive, but even her fans couldn't help noting that a woman in her mid-twenties was hard to believe in the matronly role of Dolly Levi. The soundtrack album, meanwhile, was a moderate success, getting to #49. (It was not released on CD until 1994.)

As the 1960s came to an end, Barbra Streisand's career appeared to have peaked. It had been a remarkable career, with success in records, live appearances, theater, television, and film. But in the volatile world of entertainment, Streisand, at age 27, now appeared to be dangerously old-fashioned, a big-time movie musical star at a time when movie musicals were disappearing, a traditional pop singer in an age of rock. But Streisand would find ways to turn the changing trends to her advantage and return in the '70s as successful as ever.

LEFT: **Dolly Levi enters Delmonico's in the ''Hello, Dolly!'' sequence of** *Hello, Dolly!*, **which finally opened in movie theaters in December 1969.**

RIGHT: **In Oscar etiquette, last year's Best Actress gives out this year's Best Actor Award. Here, Streisand gives John Wayne his statuette for** *True Grit*, **April 7, 1970.** *Women's Wear Daily* **called her outfit ''A nice pink bar-mitzvah-mother dress.'' ''Beginner's luck,'' Wayne whispered to her.**

THE WAY WE WERE

In February 1970, Columbia released *Barbra Streisand's Greatest Hits*, a collection of 11 singles, only two of which had reached the Top 40. It seemed to confirm that Streisand wasn't a singles artist, and its profit-taking nature seemed to be something of a kiss-off for the million-dollar recording star who was starting to look like a major debit on the company ledger. The album reached #32.

Streisand, meanwhile, was working on a new album to be called *The Singer*, based largely on ballads written by Michel Legrand and Marilyn and Alan Bergman.

With the failure of *Hello, Dolly!*, Paramount scaled down the planned three-hour extravaganza that *On A Clear Day You Can See Forever* originally was intended to be. Cut to 129 minutes (which is still long for a movie), it escaped into theaters in June 1970, and though Streisand's personal notices were often generous, it failed to make back as much as five of the $10 million that had been spent on it. The soundtrack album got to #108.

As Streisand spent her second summer singing "Second Hand Rose" to Las Vegas gamblers, therefore, her career was clearly on a downward slide. Her record sales were falling, her movies were flopping, and it might not have seemed unreasonable to think that, in Las Vegas, she had found her natural level. But that didn't turn out to be true.

Streisand put aside *The Singer* LP (which was never released, though tracks turned up on later albums) when Clive Davis suggested that she work with a young producer named Richard Perry and record a number of contemporary pop-rock songs he and Perry had selected, among them Laura Nyro's "Stoney End."

Laura Nyro had found success as a songwriter whose tunes had become hits for Blood, Sweat and Tears and The 5th Dimension and as a recording artist with the 1969 album *Eli And The Thirteenth Confession*. Somehow, nobody had discovered "Stoney End," which she had recorded on her 1966 debut album *More Than New Discovery*. Nyro had an emotive, multi-range singing style that had mostly been tamed in the cover versions of her songs. But Streisand could handle it, and her "Stoney End" (closely patterned on Nyro's original) was a triumph, the first time she was able to marry her

LEFT: As Daisy Gamble in one of the previous-life sequences in *On A Clear Day You Can See Forever*.

RIGHT: As Judy Maxwell in *What's Up, Doc?* (1972).

RIGHT: Getting the upper hand on Howard Bannister (Ryan O'Neal) in *What's Up, Doc?*

LEFT: Doris and Felix (George Segal) in *The Owl And The Pussycat* (1970).

RIGHT: Robert Tentrees (John Richardson) and Daisy Gamble in *On A Clear Day You Can See Forever*.

impassioned, full-throated singing style to a pop-rock song.

"Stoney End" was released in September. As a single release by a non-singles artist, its progress was slow. But it entered the Hot 100 by the end of October, Streisand's first listing in over three years. Eventually, it would hit #6.

In a sense, Streisand hadn't so much joined the '60s hard rockers as endured until the '70s soft rockers had emerged and then joined them. The week that "Stoney End" hit the charts, the Carpenters and James Taylor were in the Top Five, and the chart also included such names as Neil Diamond, Anne Murray, and Kenny Rogers. A new generation of pop performers had come along to replace the Sinatras and other pre-rock singers. With "Stoney End," Streisand had made the transition from the pre-Beatles era to the post-Beatles era.

Her triumph was consolidated by the November opening of *The Owl And The Pussycat*, which redefined the big musical star as a street-smart comic actress. The film grossed $12 million, and with its small budget, that made it a solid hit. Thus, as Streisand spent another stint in Las Vegas in December, she had reason to feel much better than she had back in July.

She could feel even better in February 1971, when Columbia released the *Stoney End* LP and it soared into the Top 10, going gold by April, Streisand's first album to do so well since *Color Me Barbra* five years before.

In May, it was reported that Streisand would have a role in a film called *A Glimpse Of Tiger* that had previously been intended to star her estranged husband Elliott Gould. The project underwent changes in cast, writers, and directors before emerging, in wholly unrecognizable form, as Streisand's next movie, *What's Up Doc?* Rehearsals began in July.

Meanwhile, Streisand also had been working on a follow-up to *Stoney End* with producer Richard Perry. July saw the release of the advance single "Where You Lead," a song written by Carole King and Toni Stern that had just appeared

on King's massively successful *Tapestry* album. The single hit #40. It was followed in September by *Barbra Joan Streisand*, on which the singer essayed more titles by King, plus two songs from John Lennon, an otherwise unrecorded song by

Donald Fagen and Walter Becker, who had not yet formed Steely Dan, and one by Laura Nyro. The album reached #11 after its release in August.

Streisand finished 1971 back at the Las Vegas Hilton (the renamed International). Her final appearance on January 13, 1972, would be the last time she would sing live for paying customers for nearly 22 years.

Her next appearance was on film, with the release of *What's Up Doc?* in March 1972. The film, an updated screwball comedy with strong echoes of the 1938 Cary Grant-Katharine Hepburn movie *Bringing Up Baby*, which co-starred Ryan O'Neal and was directed by Peter Bogdanovich, was a critical and commercial smash. It was Streisand's first out-and-out comic farce, and she was universally praised. Today, it still ranks among her two or three best films.

On April 15, Streisand appeared at a benefit concert called "Four for McGovern" at the Los Angeles Forum. The other three supporting the presidential candidacy of Senator George McGovern were James Taylor, Carole King, and Quincy Jones. Other than her Vegas shows, it was Streisand's first live performance in five years, and it was taped by Columbia.

In fact, only two months later, the label released a single recorded at the show, a medley of "Sweet Inspiration" and "Where You Lead" that hit #37. *Live Concert At The Forum* was in record stores just before McGovern lost the election to President Richard Nixon. It reached #19.

On December 21, Streisand's sixth film, *Up The Sandbox*, opened. It concerned a young married woman who experiences a varied set of daydreams after discovering she is pregnant. It had a vaguely feminist slant, but its good

intentions did not result in a successful work. "*Up The Sandbox* was a box-office flop," Streisand writes in her liner notes to *Just For The Record . . .* , "but I thought it was a wonderful film and I'm still very proud of it!"

That fall, Streisand had shot her seventh film. *The Way We Were* told the love story of Katie Morosky, a politically active college student of the 1930s, and Hubbell Gardiner, an apolitical campus jock with aspirations to be a writer. Streisand's co-star was Robert Redford.

In April and May 1973, Streisand cut an album of classical songs with the CBS Symphony Orchestra. But the record was shelved and wouldn't be released for three years. After finishing it, Streisand went to England to shoot her long-overdue fifth television special.

The Way We Were opened in October to overwhelming success. It earned Streisand her second Best Actress Oscar nomination and has gone down as one of her best films. The movie's theme song, written by Marvin Hamlisch and the Bergmans, was released as a single simultaneously with the film. A lush ballad expertly sung by Streisand, it became her first #1 hit and first gold single. It would win the Oscar and the Grammy for Best Song.

The TV special did not fare so well. Broadcast November 2, "Barbra Streisand . . . And Other Musical Instruments" was intended to "incorporate instruments and musical styles from all over the world," Streisand notes in *Just For The Record. . . .* Though she says "it's a show I'm proud of," especially because of guest star Ray Charles, it was widely criticized, and Streisand has not released it on home video. The soundtrack album got to #64, the lowest showing ever for a Barbra Streisand album.

Far more successful was a Columbia album entitled *Barbra Streisand Featuring The Way We Were And All In Love Is Fair* that was released in January 1974. The album looks like a rush job, throwing together many older tracks, several of them originally intended for the 1970 *The Singer* album, with a few newly recorded numbers. But that didn't matter. In the bonanza that accompanied *The Way We Were*, the album topped the charts and went gold. Meanwhile, a soundtrack album from the film hit #20.

Streisand turned back to screwball comedy for her next film *For Pete's Sake*, which concerned a young wife who gets into increasing trouble trying to help out her husband. It opened in June and proved to be one of Streisand's more forgettable vehicles, though it made money. Streisand's short wig in the film was the work of Jon Peters, who owned a string of hairdressing salons in Los Angeles. Peters and Streisand began a relationship that soon found him taking a major role in her career.

In fact, in October, when Columbia issued Streisand's next album, *ButterFly*, Peters, whose previous musical experience was unknown, was credited as the LP's producer. *ButterFly* was a return to the "contemporary" style of *Stoney End* and *Barbra Joan Streisand* and featured Bob Marley's "Guava Jelly" as well as songs by Graham Nash and David Bowie. Did anyone want to hear Barbra Streisand sing "Life On Mars"? Apparently. The album went to #13.

Streisand's next picture, which she agreed to reluctantly and due to a contractual commitment to Ray Stark, was *Funny Lady*, a *Funny Girl* sequel. It opened in March 1975. With a combination of period songs and a new score written by John Kander and Fred Ebb, it was not a memorable effort on screen or on record, though the soundtrack hit #6 and went gold.

Streisand's next album release, in October 1975, was *Lazy Afternoon*, described by critic Stephen Holden as "a winning throwback to prerock days." The LP sold to Streisand's established audience, getting to #12 and going gold, but it has not held up as one of her more impressive efforts.

Classical Barbra, pulled off the shelf and released four months later, might be described as a winning throwback to pre-*pop* days. The Columbia Masterworks release found Streisand singing the music of Debussy, Handel, Schumann and others. Not a typical Streisand release, it nevertheless reached #46 in the charts. Apparently, Columbia had been persuaded to release it because Streisand was going to be too busy for the moment to make any new records.

Her main project for 1975-1976 was a film originally called

Rainbow Road that intended to transfer the story line of *A Star Is Born*, which had been used for three previous movies, into the world of rock 'n' roll. That plot, which is strikingly similar to *Funny Girl*, concerns an up-and-coming star who marries an established star who is in decline and, in the end, dies. *Rainbow Road* went through many permutations, in one of which Streisand was to play the established star, though she eventually played the up-and-comer. At one point, Jon Peters was even set to co-star.

Eventually, the film re-acquired its original title, *A Star Is Born*, and a new co-star in Kris Kristofferson. Streisand not only starred, but also was executive producer. Peters was credited as producer. (It was around this time that Peters also supplanted Marty Erlichman as Streisand's personal manager.) When the film and its soundtrack album were released (the LP coming in November 1976, the movie in December), they met a firestorm of criticism. Pre-release news reports had detailed on-set difficulties, but the bad reviews were almost inevitable, even if everything had gone smoothly. Film critics hated *A Star Is Born* because Streisand and Peters had had the nerve to try to remake *two* film classics, the 1937 and 1954 versions. Music critics hated it because Streisand had dared to try to portray the rock music industry on film.

Filmgoers and record buyers, as is often the case, didn't

care what the critics thought. In theaters, *A Star Is Born* was a massive hit. In record stores, it did even better. Record sales were helped by the single release of "Love Theme From 'A Star Is Born' (Evergreen)," which had been co-written by Streisand and Paul Williams and which became Streisand's second gold-selling #1 hit, also going on to win a Best Song Oscar and Song of the Year and Best Arrangement Grammys. The album also hit #1. It had sold a million copies by January 21, 1977, making it Streisand's first platinum record.

Despite, or perhaps because of its enormous success, *A Star Is Born* was the last Barbra Streisand film for three years. Instead of making movies, she turned her attention back to

recording. In May 1977, Columbia released the single "My Heart Belongs To Me," which soared to #4, Streisand's first Top 10 hit in six years that was not the theme from one of her movies. The single was the advance word on her new album, *Streisand Superman*, which was released in June. The album basked in the success of *A Star Is Born* in more ways than one, its tracks including discards from the soundtrack, its liner notes thanking the fans. Doubtless some of the film's momentum helped propel it to #3 as well, making it Streisand's first non-soundtrack platinum album. (In fact, it became apparent that *A Star Is Born* had catapulted Streisand to a new level of popularity as a recording artist. From here on

PREVIOUS PAGE: As Esther Hoffman onstage in *A Star Is Born* (1976).

LEFT: Jon Peters and Streisand holding one of the three Golden Globe Awards they won for *A Star Is Born*, January 30, 1977.

BELOW: Neil Diamond and singing partner at the Grammy Awards, February 27, 1980, where they sang "You Don't Bring Me Flowers," nominated for Record of the Year; it lost to the Doobie Brothers' "What A Fool Believes," but *Billboard* said the performance was "the classiest spot in the show."

out, every album she made would sell at least a million copies.)

Songbird, released in May 1978, was the first record on Streisand's new Columbia Records contract (her third), which guaranteed her $1.5 million per album. It hit #11 (its title track becoming a #25 single), but was one of those merely professional efforts that suggested the singer was going through the motions. She followed it with a new single in July, singing the title song from a new Jon Peters-produced movie thriller, "Love Theme From 'Eyes Of Laura Mars,'" which hit #21.

It was then that disc jockey Gary Guthrie, of WAKY-AM in Louisville, Kentucky, made the discovery that both Streisand and Neil Diamond had recorded on their latest albums a ballad written by Diamond with Alan and Marilyn Bergman called "You Don't Bring Me Flowers" and that both versions were in the same key. He made a tape in which he spliced the two versions together, creating a duet. He also created a hit.

Conveniently enough, both Diamond and Streisand recorded for Columbia, so there was no contractual

ABOVE: In a clench with John Norman Howard (Kris Kristofferson) in *A Star Is Born*.

LEFT: No, this is not Barbra Streisand winning a Grammy Award. It's Esther Hoffman winning one in *A Star Is Born*, and the reason she doesn't look happy is that her drunken husband, rock star John Norman Howard, is on his way up to disrupt the proceedings.

RIGHT: As Fanny Brice in an elaborate production number in *Funny Lady*.

PREVIOUS PAGE: Eddie "Kid Natural" Scanlon (Ryan O'Neal) and his manager, Hillary Kramer, back in the ring, *The Main Event* (1979).

LEFT: O'Neal, in his sweats, and Streisand, in her aerobics outfit, in the athletically inclined *The Main Event*.

BELOW: Streisand displays the award for "Woman of Achievement in the Arts" given to her by the Anti-Defamation League in 1978.

impediment to getting the two together in a studio to cut a new version of the song. The result was a gold single that went to #1. It also helped *Barbra Streisand's Greatest Hits, Volume 2*, released in October, hit #1.

With massive ballad hits like "The Way We Were," "Evergreen," and "You Don't Bring Me Flowers," Streisand seemed to have proved herself as a contemporary artist without ever really establishing herself as a rock presence. It was at this juncture that she made the curious decision to give pop's latest fad, disco, a shot.

Streisand returned to the movie theaters as actress and co-producer in June 1979 with a romantic comedy called *The Main Event* that once again co-starred her with Ryan O'Neal. And once again, the teaming worked, with the film grossing

nearly $60 million. For the movie's theme, Streisand enlisted Paul Jabara, who had written the disco hit "Last Dance" for Donna Summer. Jabara and his co-writers turned out something fairly similar in the medley "The Main Event/Fight," which was released as a single on May 31 and appeared on the soundtrack album in three versions, one of them an 11-minute dance mix. Streisand as disco diva was embraced in the summer of 1979, as the single became a gold #3 hit, but the soundtrack album only got to a disappointing #20.

Jabara then put Streisand into a studio with Summer for another disco track, "No More Tears (Enough Is Enough)," released October 5. The duet went gold and hit #1, which helped Streisand's album *Wet*, an otherwise uneven collection of songs relating to moisture, sell in her usual numbers.

THE YESHIVA BOY

Few performers at Streisand's level have shown an interest in musical collaboration, and she herself backed into it by way of "You Don't Bring Me Flowers." After that, however, she benefitted from working with others, especially on her next project. In 1980, Streisand collaborated with another of the biggest acts of the late '70s, making an entire album of songs written by the Bee Gees. On two tracks, she duetted with co-producer Barry Gibb. The result was the most successful album of her career.

In August, the LP was prefaced by a single, "Woman In Love." Concerned that she was becoming too associated with duets, Streisand deliberately held back the title track, wishing to establish the album with a solo single. She did: "Woman In Love" hit #1. The album, *Guilty*, became an across-the-board smash, critically lauded and massively successful when it was released in September. Columbia also released the duet title track as a single, and it hit #3. *Guilty* was certified platinum in November. It went to #1 in 12 countries and sold 20 million copies worldwide, making it one of the biggest selling albums of all time. (A third single, the duet "What Kind Of Fool," was released in January 1981 and became the album's third Top 10 hit.) On February 25, Streisand and Gibb won the Grammy Award for Best Pop Performance by a Duo or Group with Vocal for the song "Guilty."

The success of the *Guilty* album closed another chapter in Streisand's career. It finally confirmed that she ranked in the world of rock, and having proved that, she largely abandoned "contemporary" music, even going so far as to apologize to her fans for this phase of her career when she was accepting her Lifetime Achievement Grammy in 1992.

She had moved on to a new ambition. As early as 1968, Streisand had among her tentative projects a film version of Isaac Bashevis Singer's short story "Yentl, The Yeshiva Boy."

ABOVE: George Dupler (Gene Hackman) and Cheryl Gibbons (Streisand as a blonde) in the ill-advised *All Night Long* (1981).

RIGHT: In the second decade of her relationship with the newly clean-cut Jon Peters, December 1982.

NEXT PAGE: Avigdor (Mandy Patinkin), Yentl, and a cast of dozens in *Yentl* (1983).

The story concerns a girl in nineteenth-century Poland who pretends to be a boy in order to become a Talmudic scholar. It sounded like a risky commercial proposition, and though Streisand periodically tried to interest movie studios, it was always rejected.

By 1981, however, Streisand finally found a home for the film at MGM/UA. By now, she was set not only to co-produce *Yentl*, but also to act in it, co-write the screenplay, and direct it. The project had also become a musical, with songs by the Bergmans and Legrand, of course, to make it more commercial.

Much of Streisand's time over the next couple of years was devoted to *Yentl*. (She did take time out to step into a supporting role in the flop film *All Night Long*, however, replacing Lisa Eichhorn after production had begun. This curious turn of events is perhaps explainable as a favor to Streisand's agent, Sue Mengers, whose husband was directing the film. Then, too, her $4 million salary couldn't have hurt.)

Meanwhile, for the 1981 Christmas season, Columbia released *Memories*, an album containing some of Streisand's biggest ballad hits plus a couple of new ones, one of which, "Comin' In And Out Of Your Life," was released as a single and hit #11. *Memories* demonstrated that Streisand retained her commercial punch by hitting the Top 10 and spending a total of two years in the charts, off and on.

Streisand spent 1982 shooting *Yentl* and much of 1983 editing it. Finally, November 1983 brought the release of the film and its soundtrack album, which had been prefaced by a single, "The Way He Makes Me Feel," released in October. The single got to #40. The album hit #9 and sold a million copies, while the film earned respectable notices and revenues, if it was not a complete knockout. Fans and foes alike had been so concerned that Streisand was overreaching that the competence with which the film was handled was itself a kind of triumph, and many wondered why Streisand did not receive an Oscar nomination for Best Director, especially after she won the Best Director Award at the Golden Globes in January 1984, which are thought of as a harbinger of the Oscars.

PREVIOUS PAGE: **The first-time director shooting** *Yentl* **in Europe, spring 1982.**

ABOVE: Mandy Patinkin as Avigdor with his fellow Yeshiva student Yentl.

LEFT: Yentl and his (her?) fiancée (!) Hadass (Amy Irving).

Streisand prepared her first new, non-soundtrack album in four years for release in the fall of 1984. *Emotion*, released in October, represented a new attempt at a "contemporary" album, featuring some old hands, such as Richard Perry and Albhy Galuten (who had co-produced *Guilty*), plus new collaborators like Earth, Wind and Fire leader Maurice White and Kim Carnes. The result was a mixed success. Streisand's records were no longer automatic monster sellers, though she maintained her established floor of about a million copies per release.

By 1985, if it had become more difficult for established non-rap, non-heavy metal performers like Streisand to hit the top of the charts, there nevertheless remained an adult audience that was proving receptive to a variety of sophisticated, somewhat retro sounds, especially if they were packaged well. Linda Ronstadt had succeeded with a series of albums of standards, and new non-rock performers like Harry Connick, Jr., and Michael Feinstein also were gaining a hearing.

Streisand chose this time, apparently over considerable record company opposition, to record an album of show tunes, something many of her long-time fans had always thought she was at her best doing. The result was the surprise hit of the 1985 Christmas season and one of the biggest albums of Barbra Streisand's career.

ABOVE: With Stephen Sondheim during the making of *The Broadway Album* (1985), which featured many of his songs, some of them rewritten to Streisand's specifications.

RIGHT: With Leonore Gershwin, widow of Ira Gershwin, backstage at the Grammy Awards, February 25, 1986, after Streisand had presented Gershwin with the Grammys' National Trustees Award to honor her husband and his brother George.

NEXT PAGE: With Congresswoman Bella Abzug at a fund-raiser for Abzug held at Streisand's home in Beverly Hills in July 1976. Streisand was a long-time supporter of Abzug, dating back to 1970.

Perhaps the best decision in a dream project was to build the album around the songs of Stephen Sondheim. Surprisingly, Streisand had avoided the work of Broadway's best living composer. Now, she cherry-picked tunes from among his shows, even getting him to fill in some lyrics for his most famous song, "Send In The Clowns." Sondheim also rewrote his "Putting It Together" to turn it into a commentary on the troubles Streisand was having marshalling support for the album.

Streisand found space for songs from *Guys and Dolls, Porgy and Bess, The King and I, Show Boat, Carousel,* and *West Side Story.* If *The Broadway Album* isn't the best record she ever made, it's a close second. And so it was perceived upon release in November 1985. It shot to #1, staying in the charts almost a year and selling three million copies. Eventually, the album won Streisand another Best Pop Vocal Performance, Female, Grammy.

On January 1, 1986, Marty Erlichman returned to Streisand as her "business associate," replacing Jon Peters, with whom she had broken up romantically some time before.

The singer had always been an outspoken advocate for liberal causes and a supporter of the Democratic Party, and on September 6, 1986, for the first time in more than 14 years, she performed a concert once again to raise funds for the campaign of California Senator Alan Cranston and others. But she didn't leave home. Instead, she invited 300 friends to her ranch in Malibu and charged them $5000 each to listen. The result was *One Voice,* filmed and recorded, which turned up as a special on the HBO cable television network in December and was released as an album by Columbia in April 1987. The album, all of whose proceeds went to the newly formed charity organization, the Streisand Foundation, hit #9. (The Streisand Foundation has since donated millions of dollars to environmental concerns, AIDS research, and other causes.)

Streisand seemed to have left her "kook" image long behind her, but starting on November 20, 1987, she played the film role of a character who may or may not be *Nuts,* as the title of the Martin Ritt-directed picture had it. In a moving dramatic character part, Streisand gave one of her best performances. She also produced the film and wrote the score, which was released by Columbia as a 13-minute mini-album on December 21.

The vocal theme from the movie, "Two People," with lyrics by the Bergmans, didn't turn up on record until a year later, when Streisand released her first new LP since *The Broadway Album* and her first album of all-new songs in four years. This was *Till I Loved You.* The title song was a duet with Streisand's current boyfriend, TV actor Don Johnson.

PREVIOUS PAGE: **Streisand speaking at a pro-choice rally in Rancho Park, California, on November 12, 1989.**

ABOVE: **With Richard Dreyfuss in *Nuts* (1987).**

LEFT: **With singing and romantic partner Don Johnson at Bally's in Las Vegas, February 24, 1988.**

Released as a single on October 6, 1986, it hit #25. The album, which followed on October 25, was, like *Emotion*, a multi-producer affair with a wide variety of musical approaches and styles. An automatic Top 10 and million seller, it was nonetheless not among Streisand's best records.

In October 1989, Columbia released another repackaging, *A Collection: Greatest Hits . . . And More*, which contained 10 previously released songs (two of them cannibalized from the last compilation, *Memories*), plus two new songs, "We're Not Makin' Love Anymore," a co-composition by Michael Bolton and Diane Warren (for better or worse, two of the most successful pop songwriters of their day) and "Someone That I Used To Love," by Michael Masser and Gerry Goffin. The album only reached #26.

ORDINARY MIRACLES

If there were any doubt about Streisand's ongoing commercial clout, it was erased when Columbia released *Just For The Record . . .* in September 1991. The four-CD boxed set differed from most of the retrospective collections that have become career benchmarks for well-known performers. This one was compiled and annotated by Streisand herself, and, with four hits albums in print, she opted to turn it into a scrapbook for fans, filling it with previously unreleased songs, TV performances, and demos.

Just For The Record . . . was a gift, albeit at a hefty price, to Streisand's die-hard fans. Apparently there were quite a few of them: in the flood of boxed sets released in the fall of 1991, it was the best seller of the bunch, hitting #38 and going platinum.

The singer herself, meanwhile, had hit the interview circuit with a vengeance, submitting herself to the scrutiny of everyone from *Vanity Fair* magazine, which puffed her up and put her on the cover, to CBS's "60 Minutes" TV show, whose Mike Wallace (her old host from "PM East") pilloried her and put her down. All of this was in the service of promoting her latest film, *The Prince Of Tides*, in which she co-starred with Nick Nolte and which she had directed and co-produced.

RIGHT: President-elect Bill Clinton administers one of his famous big hugs to Barbra Streisand the night before his inauguration and just after her performance at his gala at the Capital Centre in Landover, Maryland, January 19, 1993.

NEXT PAGE: Streisand shows off her Grammy Living Legends Award to reporters, February 25, 1992.

ABOVE: Tom Wingo (Nick Nolte) dances with his sister's psychiatrist in *The Prince Of Tides* (1991).

RIGHT: Setting up a shot on *The Prince Of Tides* set, Beaufort, South Carolina, 1990.

Released for Christmas, the film was well-received, though Streisand was again denied a Best Director Oscar nomination. The soundtrack album, with a score by James Newton Howard, also featured two new Streisand vocals, "For All We Know" and "Places That Belong To You," that were not actually heard in the film.

Streisand kept a relatively low profile during 1992, though she made news politically, helping out the successful presidential campaign of Bill Clinton. The November election not only brought Clinton in, however, but also success to a referendum in Colorado that banned anti-discrimination laws protecting gay people that had been enacted in several cities in the state. An outraged Streisand spoke out in favor of a boycott of Colorado, which is a favorite ski vacation spot for Hollywood stars. (The ban was held to be unconstitutional by the Colorado State Supreme Court in October 1994.)

On January 19, 1993, a series of musical performers and actors turned up onstage at the Capital Centre in Landover, Maryland, in a pre-Inaugural Gala to herald the coming of Bill

Clinton's presidency. Each had one song on the TV broadcast except Michael Jackson, who sang two songs and gave a moving speech about AIDS. But the last 15 minutes of the broadcast belonged to Streisand, who sang three songs ("Evergreen," Sondheim's "Children Will Listen," and "America The Beautiful"), talked about child abuse, drank tea, and invited the new president up onstage. It was hard to miss the point that she was the biggest star of the evening.

Streisand's continuing clout in record stores was demonstrated by the June release of *Back To Broadway*, her follow-up to *The Broadway Album*, which jumped to #1 in its first week of release and quickly sold a million copies.

During her interviews for *The Prince Of Tides*, Streisand had spoken of the possibility of touring again. In October 1993 it was announced that she would perform two concerts, on New Year's Eve and New Year's Day, at the new MGM Grand Hotel in Las Vegas. Streisand put on an elaborate show, complete with an autobiographical story line that found her talking to an invisible psychiatrist and showing scenes from her movies, as well as singing her greatest hits.

The scale of the show suggested more than a two-night stand, so it was no surprise when it was announced that Streisand would tour. Tickets went on sale in March 1994 for the 26 shows, which would begin in London in April and end

PREVIOUS PAGE, ABOVE: With U.N. ambassador Madeleine Albright. The two were together to host a luncheon honoring the U.S. delegation to the 37th session of the Commission on the Status of Women, April 23, 1993.

PREVIOUS PAGE, BELOW: With New York Mayor David Dinkins at a re-election rally shortly before Dinkins's loss to Rudolph Giuliani, October 27, 1993.

ABOVE: With Barbara Walters of ABC-TV's "20/20," with whom she discussed her upcoming Las Vegas shows. November 10, 1993.

LEFT: With Presidential counsel Lloyd Cutler at a State Dinner for the Japanese emperor.

(after a few postponements due to laryngitis) in July in Anaheim. They sold out instantly, of course, though there was controversy due to the top ticket price of $350, which made for a gross of $70 million. (A large block of seats were sold to charities, which were allowed to resell them for up to $1000.)

During the tour, Columbia released a new Streisand single, "Ordinary Miracles," which she was singing in her shows. It was contained in a subsequent album, *Barbra: The Concert*. Released in September, the album sold nearly 100,000 copies in its first week and entered the charts at #10. Prior to that, Streisand assembled a TV special of the tour, which ran on HBO in August and became its highest rated program ever.

The future for Streisand already has some vague outlines. For recordings, she has mentioned *The Hollywood Album*, a collection of tunes from the movies. And there will certainly be more films. These could include a mother-daughter story called *The Mirror Has Two Faces* and a long-promised adaptation of Larry Kramer's play about the AIDS crisis, *The Normal Heart*. Another, less definite film project is a biography of the photojournalist Margaret Bourke-White.

All these possibilities suggest that the most amazing aspect of an amazing career may be that the woman Stephen Holden has called "the most influential mainstream American pop singer since Frank Sinatra" may, at the age of 52, be not much more than halfway through that career.

ABOVE, LEFT: With Oscar winners Jack Nicholson (Best Actor) and Clint Eastwood (Best Picture) at the 1992 Academy Awards, March 29, 1993.

TOP: At the Women in Film "Crystal Awards" at the Beverly Hilton Hotel in Beverly Hills, June 11, 1992.

ABOVE: With playwright Larry Kramer at a staged reading of his play *The Normal Heart* (to which she owns film rights), Criterion Center, New York City, April 16, 1993.

RIGHT: Onstage at the U.S. Air Arena in Landover, Maryland, May 10, 1994.

DISCOGRAPHY

(M) = Mono   (S) = Stereo

Record #	Title	Year
Columbia		
KOL-5780 (M)	I Can Get It For You	1962
KOS-2180 (S)	Wholesale: Broadway Cast	
OL-5810 (M)	Pins And Needles: Studio	1962
OS-2210 (S)	Cast	
CL-2007 (M)	The Barbra Streisand Album	1963
CS-8807 (S)	The Barbra Streisand Album	1963
CL-2054 (M)	The Second Barbra	1963
CS-8854 (S)	Streisand Album	
CL-2154 (M)	The Third Album	1964
CS-8954 (S)	The Third Album	1964
Capitol		
VAS-2059 (M)	Funny Girl: Broadway Cast	1964
SVAS-2059 (S)	Funny Girl: Broadway Cast	1964
Columbia		
CL-2215 (M)	People	1964
CS-9015 (S)	People	1964
CL-2336 (M)	My Name Is Barbra	1965
CS-9136 (S)	My Name Is Barbra	1965
CL-2409 (M)	My Name Is Barbra, Two . . .	1965
CS-9209 (S)	My Name Is Barbra, Two . . .	1965
CL-2478 (M)	Color Me Barbra	1966
CS-9278 (S)	Color Me Barbra	1966
2920	Harold Sings Arlen (With Friend): Harold Arlen (The friend is Barbra Streisand.)	1966
CL-2547 (M)	Je M'Appelle Barbra	1966
CS-9347 (S)	Je M'Appelle Barbra	1966
CL-2682 (M)	Simply Streisand	1967
CS-9482 (S)	Simply Streisand	1967
CL-2757 (M)	A Christmas Album	1967
CS-9557 (S)	A Christmas Album	1967
BOS-3220	Funny Girl (Soundtrack)	1968
CS-9710	A Happening In Central Park	1968
CS-9816	What About Today?	1969
20th Century-Fox		
DTCS 5103	Hello, Dolly! (Soundtrack)	1969
Columbia		
CS-9968	Barbra Streisand's Greatest Hits	1970
S-30086	On A Clear Day You Can See Forever: Soundtrack	1970
S-30401	The Owl And The Pussycat: Soundtrack	1971
PC 30378	Stoney End	1971
KC 30792	Barbra Joan Streisand	1971
KC 31760	Live Concert At The Forum	1972
KC 32655	Barbra Streisand . . . And Other Musical Instruments	1973
JC 32801	Barbra Streisand Featuring The Way We Were And All In Love Is Fair	1974
32830	The Way We Were: Soundtrack	1974
PC 33095	ButterFly	1974

Record #	Title	Year
Arista		
AL 9004	Funny Lady (Soundtrack)	1975
Columbia		
PC 33815	Lazy Afternoon	1975
M 33452	Classical Barbra	1976
JS 34403	A Star Is Born (Soundtrack)	1976
JC 34830	Streisand Superman	1977
PC 35375	Songbird	1978
FC 35679	Barbra Streisand's Greatest Hits, Volume 2	1978
JS 36115	The Main Event (Soundtrack)	1979
FC 36258	Wet	1979
FC 36750	Guilty	1980
TC 37678	Memories	1981
JS 39152	Yentl (Soundtrack)	1983
OC 39480	Emotion	1984
OC 40092	The Broadway Album	1985
CK 40788	One Voice	1987
40876	Nuts: Soundtrack (composed by Streisand)	1987
OC 40880	Till I Loved You	1988
OC 45369	A Collection: Greatest Hits . . . And More	1989
C4K 44111	Just For The Record . . .	1991
CK 48627	The Prince Of Tides (Soundtrack)	1991
CK 52849	Just For The Record . . . (abridged version)	1992
CK 44189	Back To Broadway	1993
C2K 66109	Barbra – The Concert Recorded Live At Madison Square Garden	1994

LEFT: **Best Pop Vocalist Grammy Award, 1987.**

Index

ACKNOWLEDGMENTS
The publisher would like to thank Mike Rose for designing this book, Caroline Earle for editing it, Rita Longabucco for the picture research, Nicki Giles for production, and Ron Watson for compiling the index. The following agencies provided photographic material:

Archive Photos: Pictorial Parade: page 27
Brompton Photo Library: pages 6, 7, 9(both), 10, 21, 29(top), 33, 36, 37, 38, 39, 40(both), 43, 44(top left), 45(bottom right), 46(both), 48, 50(bottom), 51, 52, 53(left), 54(top), 55, 56, 57(both), 58(top), 59, 61(top), 64(both), 65(top), 70
Ron Galella, Inc: Gustavo Castilla: page 1; **Ron Galella:** pages 34(top right, bottom), 35, 47(bottom), 49(both), 53(right), 54(bottom); **Albert Ortega:** pages 8, 65(bottom), 68(top right); **Anthony Savignano:** pages 66(bottom), 68(bottom right); **James Smeal:** pages 4-5, 11, 60, 61(bottom), 68(top left)
London Features, International: George De Sota: pages 2-3
National Film Archive, London: pages 41, 50(top)
Reuters/Bettmann Newsphotos: pages 62, 63, 66(top), 67(both), 69
UPI/Bettmann Newsphotos: pages 12, 13, 14, 15, 16(both), 17, 18, 19, 20, 22, 23, 24, 25, 26(both), 28, 29(bottom), 30, 31(both), 32, 34(top left), 44-45(bottom center), 47(top), 58(bottom)